Jesmond Grech

BRITISH HERITAGE IN MALTA

Miller Distributors Limited
Miller House, Tarxien Road, Airport Way, Luqa Malta.
P.O. Box 25 Malta International Airport LQA 05
Telephone: 21664488 Facsimile: 21676799

CENTRO STAMPA EDITORIALE

PERSEUS

The RAF Malta Memorial, Floriana.

INTRODUCTION

*A*s a British newcomer to these beautiful islands resident since September 2002, I have enjoyed reading this book, and have learned from it. I hope you will enjoy it too.

The ties between the United Kingdom and Malta are indissoluble. They run deep, go back centuries, and are founded on mutual respect in good times and bad. This book touches on the Great Siege of Malta of 1565. Although Henry VIII took against the English League of the Order of the Knights of St. John in 1534, there was one English knight – Sir Oliver Starkey – alongside Grand Master de la Valette throughout the siege.

The author, Jesmond Grech, rightly dwells on the period from 1800, when the Royal Navy and the people of Malta struck up a friendship which was built to last throughout and beyond the period of British rule, and which embraced the Army and the RAF, through the dark years of World War II and to the present day.

Today, Malta's self-evident European vocation and Britain's continuing friendship go hand in hand. Among the visible signs are the English language, education choices, tourism, culture – including football – trade and investment. Not to mention Leyland buses, red pillar boxes and phone kiosks, and an abiding affection for things British. But it is the ties of family, affinity and friendship which make the relationship come alive.

In chronicling some of the visible signs of the British presence in Malta down the centuries, Jesmond Grech does us a service, underlining the diversity and strength of so many individual Maltese and British contributions to a living, and lively, relationship.

Vincent Fean
British High Commissioner

BRITISH HERITAGE IN MALTA

CONTENTS

Outline of Maltese History up to the British Arrival in 1800

Because of the similarities in the designs on pottery ware, archaeologists believe that the first inhabitants of the islands must have come from Sicily.

The prehistory of the Maltese islands started round about 4000 BC but it is from the period classified as the Copper Age that we have the richest and most spectacular heritage of the local prehistoric era.

During that phase we witness the development of the Temple culture, a name which was coined as a result of the substantial number of impressive megalithic temples erected in honour of a deity referred to as the "Fat Lady". Statuettes of this fertility goddess, in whose forms the temples were probably constructed, were found in Malta. However similar representations were also found throughout other countries in the Mediterranean region.

The marvellous artistry and stonemasonry with which these temples were built bear witness to the devotion which the early Maltese had to their protective goddess.

The huge upright rocks (weighing tons) which constitute the Ġgantija temples in Gozo together with the minute carving on the decorative slabs at Tarx-

Impressive boulders forming the side of Ġgantija.

Artefacts from temples.

*The islet of Fifla as seen
from the temple of Ħaġar Qim.*

*Sleeping "goddess of fertility",
The National Museum of Archaeology, Valletta.*

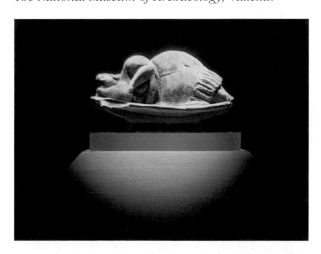

Statuette of obese figure may suggest a fertility cult.

Head of idol at The National Museum of Archaeology, Valletta.

Remnants of massive statue from Tarxien Temples.

Prehistoric idols.

Stone altar with palm-tree motif from Ħaġar Qim.

ien and Ħaġar Qim reflect the dedication with which these prehistoric ancestors adorned their places of worship. Yet the Hypogeum in Paola remains the most astonishing site of the temple builders. Discovered by accident in 1902, the excavation works were carried out by Malta's leading archaeologist, Sir Themistocles Zammit. Using only flint and rock tools (some of which were unearthed during the excavation) the Neolithic people dug an underground temple in live rock, a construction which was later used as a burial place.

Perhaps the so-called "cart-ruts" are the strangest legacy from those misty, prehistoric times. Dispersed in various places in Malta and Gozo, these mysterious designs have puzzled archaeologists and scientists alike.

People have offered all sorts of explanations ranging from tracks formed by primitive forms of animal-driven machinery to signs from an extra-terrestrial culture!

Around 800 BC, the temple builders came into contact with the Phoenicians, a prosperous nation of merchants from

Ġgantija Temples, Xagħra, Gozo.

Remains of the structure of Ħaġar Qim.

Preceding pages: Tarxien Temples.

Tyre and Sidon who moved westwards colonising parts of the North African coast and founding Carthage in the process.

Commerce and trade were their only driving force and the islanders were amongst the many who must have been spellbound by their purple-dyed cloth. Eventually the Carthaginians began to pose a substantial menace to the Roman supremacy in the Mediterranean. During the course of the three Punic Wars (at the end of which Carthage was, literally, razed to the ground), Malta changed hands.

In 218 BC, following an invasion led by the Roman Consul Titus Sempronius, Malta fell under Roman rule.

The most celebrated heritage of the Roman period in Malta is the town-house (misnomerly referred to as the "Roman Villa") at Rabat, now the Museum of Roman Antiquities. However, there is also evidence of a number of temples dedicated to idols such as Apollo, Proserpine and Juno.

The most significant event which occurred during this period was the arrival of St. Paul in AD 60.

The event, recorded in the *Acts of the Apostles*, left its indelible mark on subsequent generations. Although for a while the inhabitants continued to frequent their pagan temples, Christianity progressively flourished until it was brought to an abrupt end by the Arabs.

The lack of archaeological and written material from the period of Arab rule does not help us to establish with certainty what happened to the Maltese during the Arab domination reputably starting from 800 to 1091 AD. Recent

*Massive altars from
Hagar Qim.*

*Voluminous bowl possibly
for ritual cleansing.*

*Entrance to
Hagar Qim Temple.*

documents have advanced the theory that Malta was almost totally depopulated by a hostile, invasive force which, for a while, left it in a semi-deserted state. A few years prior to the arrival of the conqueror, Count Roger of Normandy, in 1091, the islands might have been colonised by a group of people of Arab stock coming from North Africa. Until the early years of the 16th century the islands were politically dependent on the rulers of Sicily and the repercussions of what happened in Southern Italy were usually felt in Malta as well. The arrival of King Alfonso V of Aragon in 1432 was quite an unusual event, he being the first monarch ever to set foot on the islands.

During his short visit, (in which he stayed at the Inguanez Palace at Imdina), King Alfonso granted the islanders' desire to form part of the *regio demanio* (the royal domains) and so the inhabitants were accountable to him alone. The islands were governed by an elected assembly known as the *università*, which administered the everyday running of Malta in the king's name. Taxes were collected and sent to his representative, the Viceroy in Sicily. In return, the Maltese benefited by receiving the king's protection and his solemn promise that the islands will not be given as fief to his vassals.

This promise was, however, broken in 1530 when Charles V of Aragon handed the islands, together with the castle of Tripoli, to the Sovereign Military Order of St. John.

Unexplainable man-made grooves, known as "curt ruts".

THE KNIGHTS

The Knights had been expelled from Rhodes in 1522 by their eternal enemies, the Ottoman Turks and they had been seeking a base from where they could continue their relentless attacks on the Infidels.

With a military and hospitallier Order based in Malta, the population felt much safer.

The Knights started to fortify the area around the Grand Harbour where they had their galleys and built their auberges in Vittoriosa. The Turks however, had been preparing for a great invasion - an offensive which materialised in May 1565 when the Great Siege commenced. The celebrated victory over the Turks on the 8th September 1565 forged the islanders with their rulers and heralded a new period of prosperity. The Knights

St. Paul's Cave, Rabat.

Amphorae
from Punic-Roman times.

Museum of Roman Antiquities,
Rabat.

Olive-press from Roman times.

Marble head
of Roman dignitary.

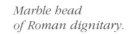

invested in the islands starting with the colossal project of the building of Valletta and a string of fortifications protecting the harbour area and the coast. During the 268 years of administration under the Order of St. John the Maltese enjoyed prosperous periods and the population continued to increase almost continuously. Being a naval power, the Order built ship-building and ship-repairing facilities which were later to be modernised by the British.

The Maltese were experienced seamen and many worked in the lucrative corsairing business and other related industries.

The artistic and cultural lives of the islands also flourished with the influx of artists such as Caravaggio, Mattia Preti and Favray (amongst many others) who were commissioned by the Knights to embellish churches, palaces and auberges.

For many years the grandiose fortification projects were the source of income to many Maltese but towards the

Courtyard of Norman House.
MDINA

Inner rooms of medieval house.

Courtyard of Norman House.
MDINA

late 18th century the Order of St. John was losing its touch with the population in general. Gradually it increasingly became an anachronistic institution composed of degenerate knights. It is in this context that the French Revolution sounded the death knell of the Order in Malta. Knights occupying influential positions within the Order of St. John were secretly conspiring with the French Directory and there was sufficient discontent amongst the islanders so that when Napoleon Bonaparte invaded the islands in 1798, the Maltese hailed him as their saviour and offered little resistance. Napoleon had promised liberty, equality and fraternity, but, to their horror, the Maltese soon realised that these were merely vague promises. The Inquisition was abolished and the liberty of the press was introduced but these measures masked the crude reality that Mal-

Corridors of Magisterial (now Presidential) Palace, Valletta.

ta was an occupied nation and had to bear the brunt of foreign domination. After only a few months of French administration the Maltese rebelled and managed to block the enemy in the harbour cities. It was during this insurrection that Admiral Nelson was asked to intervene so that the blockade would be a success. As early as 1798 the British fleet blockaded the Grand Harbour together with ships from other nations until General Vaubois capitulated in September 1800. During those two trying years, the Maltese and their leaders realised that peace and prosperity would ensue if the islands were to be kept under Britain's protection. The Treaty of Paris (1814) confirmed Malta a British Crown Colony and for the following 150 years Malta formed part of the Empire. Although independence was achieved on the 21st September 1964 and the islands did not continue to serve as a NATO base after the 31st March 1979, the friendship which had been forged between the two nations continued to grow.

The influence of the British on the Maltese way of life is evident in many aspects. The British systems of administration, education, and legislation were adopted and adapted by the islanders. During the years of British governorship the foundation stones were laid so that Malta could become a modern state. This book lists but a few places of interest which immediately bring back to mind the British presence on the islands.

The Armoury, Valletta.

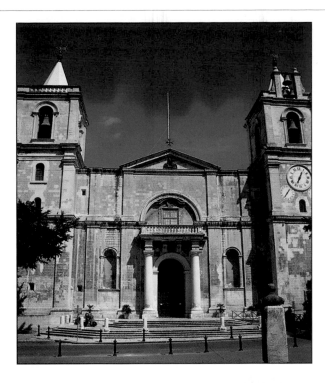

*Facade of St. John's
Co-Cathedral.*

*St. John's Co-Cathedral:
Main altar in precious marble.*

*Caravaggio's "St. Jerome" - St. John's
Co-Cathedral.*

*Co-Cathedral's museum housing
the "arazzi".*

*Following pages: "The Beheading
of St. John" by Caravaggio.*

Preceding page:
St. George and the Dragon
by Francesco Potenzano.

Works of art housed at Co-Cathedral's museum.

Entrance to Fort
St. Elmo.

Works of art housed
at Co-Cathedral's museum.

Impregnable fortifications of Valletta.

Works of art housed at Co-Cathedral's museum.

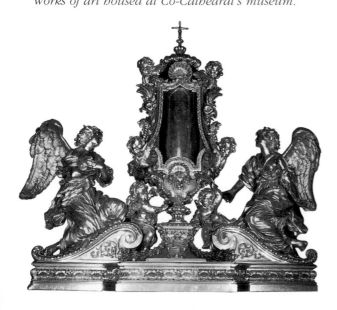

*Marble plaque commemorating
Independence Day
on 21st September 1964,
Presidential Palace, Valletta.*

Monument to Mikiel Anton Vassalli, at Żebbuġ.

*Auberge de Castille. Used as British Army
Headquarters, today the offices
of the Prime Minister.*

*List of Civil Commissioners and Governors of Malta
(1799-1964). The Palace, Valletta.*

*Monument to Dun Mikiel Xerri and fellow
countrymen, shot by the French in 1799, at
Valletta - Independence Square.*

The British Administration of Malta

On the 5th September 1800, almost two years since the Maltese revolt against their French overlords started, an armistice was signed near the Portes des Bombes, Floriana. General Claude Henri Vaubois and Rear-Admiral Pierre Villeneuve signed for France whilst Major-General Henry Pigot and Captain George Martin signed on behalf of King George III. The French had finally capitulated and they were compelled to leave the islands.

The fact that there were no representatives of His Majesty the King of the Two Sicilies was highly significant. This omission meant that the French had been defeated by the British alone. Even Captain Alexander John Ball, who had been chosen by the Maltese as their chief and representative, had been conveniently left out from the signing of the capitulation. Captain Alexander John Ball of the Royal Navy had been sent to Malta by Admiral Nelson to block the French troops in Valletta. The Maltese took a special liking to him and appointed him President of their National Assembly which he styled as "*Congresso*". The members of the Congress had, in fact, administered the day to day ongoings of the Maltese during the two years of the blockade.

The ensuing years were ones of indecision and uncertainty. Diplomats were at loggerheads when it came to determine the responsibility of the administration of the islands. When the islands had been given as fief to the Order of St. John in 1530, it had been stipulated that were the Knights to be expelled, the islands would form part of the Kingdom of the Two Sicilies. Moreover his Sicilian Majesty had not forgotten his obligation towards the Maltese and sent them help during their rebellion against the French. His was not a demand that could be easily overriden.

Yet British help during the blockade had proved instrumental in ousting the French Revolutionary troops. The latter had surrendered to the British and therefore, it could be argued that Malta was theirs by right of conquest.

The situation was very dramatic and the fate of the Maltese was determined by events in the Continent.

At the beginning of the 19th century, the British were rather tired fighting against Napoleon. The Adrington administration was seeking peace at all costs and the Treaty of Amiens was signed in 1802. Article Ten of this treaty (described by Samuel Taylor Coleridge as a "strange" treaty) provided for the evacuation of British troops in Malta and the return of the Order of St. John. Britain also agreed to relinquish Minorca, Elba and Corfu thus greatly undermining its presence in the Mediterranean.

The Treaty of Amiens was a severe blow for the Maltese who had hoped that stronger ties would be forged with the Empire. During the two years of the blockade they had grown accustomed to British protection and the presence of the Royal Navy would surely bring prosperity to the islands. In this context, a Maltese deputation was sent to King George III declaring their allegiance to the British crown and demanding the recognition of their traditional privileges and the re-establishment of the *Consiglio Popolare*.

The importance of Malta was stressed by Napoleon himself. The British Ambassador Whitworth reported that Napoleon was furious at the slow pace with which things were moving in Malta. He wanted the British out immediately. The British Ambassador stated that "He (Napoleon) placed in the front line our not evacuating Malta and Alexandria. In this, he said, no consideration on earth would make him acquiesce and of the two he would rather see us in possession of the Faubourg S. Antoine than Malta... His purpose was evi-

Portes des Bombes, Floriana.

Following pages:
typical Maltese "dgħajsa".

Sir Alexander Ball.

Coat of arms of Great Britain at
the entrance to the Old University,
Valletta. "The Gateway to
Honour is Wisdom".

The Old University, interior corridor.

dently to convince me that on Malta must depend peace or war." Luckily, there was a change of heart with regards to Malta in these crucial years. Its importance had not been immediately recognised. At first Nelson had said that keeping the islands was "a useless and enormous expense". Later he declared that he began to "consider Malta as a most important outwork to India, that it will give us (the British) great influence in the Levant and indeed all the southern parts of Italy. In this view I hope we shall never give it up." Many concurred.

Finally a decision was taken and Malta was to be kept as a naval base. As a result, hostilities were resumed on the 16th May, 1803. Sir Alexander Ball, who had been sent to supervise the evacuation of British troops, was secretly instructed to thwart the evacuation process. Ball was, by now, Civil Commissioner of the islands and, aided by his zest and good judgement, Malta benefited from a period of economic prosperity and social stability. Sir Hildebrand Oakes was appointed Civil Commissioner following Ball's death on the 25th October 1809. A portrait of Oakes still hangs at the National Library because it was through his efforts that the building retained its original purpose. Some

Keeping watch on the Grand Harbour. A watch-post known as the "Gardjola".

Grand Harbour view.

Coat of arms of Great Britain at the Main Guard. Palace Square, Valletta.

officers had had the idea of using the Library (today housing the national archives) as an officers' mess.

After the defeat of Napoleon, the Treaty of Paris (1814), officially recognised the Maltese islands as pertaining to the British Empire. The monument at the Main Guard shows the following inscription: *"Magnae et Invictae Britanniae; Melitensium Amor et Europae Vox, has Insulas Confirmat. A.D. 1814"* (To the Invincible Great Britain; Through the Love of the Maltese and the Consent of Europe, these Islands were Given. A.D. 1814).

Sir Thomas Maitland, the first Lieutenant Governor arrived on the islands on the 4th October 1813 in the midst of an outbreak of bubonic plague. The 1813 epidemic was one of the greatest of its kind to be experienced by the islanders. As a result more than 4,600 people lost their lives. Many were hastily buried in small cemeteries such as the one at Ta' Brija, in Siġġiewi and the cart in which corpses were carried (still preserved at the Zabbar Sanctuary Muse-

um) serves as a grim reminder of the ruthlessness and dehumanising conditions in which people lived during those dreadful months.

The plague completely disrupted the economic and social lives of the islanders and many years had to pass until life normalised and business began to thrive once more.

The British realised the importance of maintaining cordial relations with the local ecclesiastical authorities in view of the influence which priests exercised over the mainly rural population. Changes were never sudden or too radical but gradual and almost imperceptible. In a closely knit society such as the Maltese, moleholes could easily grow into mountains.

When the right of sanctuary was revoked on the 10th April 1828, the Chief Secretary, Sir Frederick Hankey, had to be sent on a special mission to Rome. Permission was taken from higher authorities so that the local bishop would have no choice but to obey superior orders. Up to this day, one can still see a

*Royal Commissioner Sir Hildebrand Oakes
at the National Library, Valletta.*

Burial cart used in 1813 plague at Żabbar.

*Plague cemetery
at Ta' Brija, Siġġiewi.*

*Cape Sorrel, "il-Ħaxixa Ingliża"
(lit. English grass).*

The Drydocks proved to be invaluable for British shipping.

small marble slab, placed on the facade of some wayside chapels with the words: *"Non Gode l'Immunità Ecclesia"* (Does not offer Sanctuary). Henceforth no criminal could seek the protection of the Church.

A walk in the countryside will also remind you of the British presence in Malta. From the end of November to April one can see meadows or the sides of pathways littered with yellow flowers, scientifically referred to as *Oxalis pes-caprae*. The Maltese call this plant *Qarsu* or *ħaxixa ingliża* (literally, "English grass").

It is associated with the British because its copious presence was reported in the early years of the 19th century. It is thought that the plant had been imported from South Africa where it is called Cape Sorrel. Since the presence of this beautiful plant coincided with the presence of the new colonisers, the

Maltese quickly gave it a name which would remind them of the British for ever.

With the acquisition of Malta, the British had gained an indispensable Mediterranean naval base. The Grand Harbour area, especially the dockyard, was given the utmost consideration. As technological developments constantly increased the size and speed of ships, the Admiralty invested in the modernisation of the harbour facilities. With the opening of the Suez Canal (1869) the naval traffic which passed through Malta on its way to or from India multiplied considerably. Consequently two docks, the Somerset Dock (1871) and the Hamilton Dock (1892) were constructed to meet the demands of heavier shipping.

At Vittoriosa one can still see the hub of the Victualling Yard, the Naval Bakery. In this place the Navy's daily bread supplies were prepared by the use of steam-powered machinery. The building was constructed according to the design of William Scamp, a British architect and military engineer, between 1842 and 1845. Previously, the site served as the covered slipways from which the Order's ships were launched. Presently the building is the premises of the Maritime Museum and houses an interesting collection of naval memorabilia from Punic to modern times.

In 1903 the construction of the breakwaters at the entrance of the Grand Harbour was commenced. The foundation stone of this project was laid by King Edward VII himself on April 20th 1903. Work on this massive construction project was to provide the livelihood to hundreds of workers and their families for the next three years. Consequently, the initial years of the 20th century augured well. Things, however, began to turn sour both in the local and international scene. Politically, the Maltese had clamoured for more in-volvement in local affairs practically since the beginning of British rule. In 1835 Giorgio Mitrovich, a politician from Senglea, went to London to present a petition whereby he demanded the re-establishment of the *Consiglio Popolare*, the Liberty of the Press and the reorganisation of the judiciary system on British lines especially with the introduction of trial by jury. Mitrovich was not alone in his efforts to secure more political and constitutional liberties for his countrymen. A nucleus of Maltese politically-interested personalities, including the pro-French liberal Camillo Sceberras and the Marquis Nicolo Testaferata de Noto, had joined forces to form the *Comitato Generale Maltese*. Mitrovich did not manage to actualise what the petitioners wanted. However, whilst in Britain, he had met the Liberal politician William Ewart who helped the Maltese cause as much as he could in Parliament. With the help of Ewart and a group of sympathisers, Giorgio Mitrovich managed to publish a

Breakwater at the mouth of Grand Harbour.

pamphlet entitled *"The Claims of the Maltese founded upon the Principles of Justice"*.

A short work with a long title, this publication succeeded in drawing a considerable amount of attention, so much so that during the following year, a Royal Commission was sent to the islands to investigate whether the demands of Mitrovich and his colleagues were justified.

The constitutional history of Malta during the 19th century is a series of so-called Councils of Government in which members elected by the Maltese vied for power with others chosen officially by the British Government. It was, in reality, a question of which side was to have a majority in the Council. The 1849 Constitution was the first one in which the elected element was introduced even though kept in a minority. The member elected to represent Gozo on the Council of Government was a young lawyer with a brilliant future. Dr. (later Sir) Adrian Dingli began a distinguished career during which he was appointed Crown Advocate, Knight Commander of the Order of St. Michael and St. George as well as serving on many important diplomatic missions abroad.

In 1878 two Royal Commisioners, Sir Penrose Julyan and Patrick J. Keenan, visited Malta and produced their controversial reports by which the use of English above Italian was promoted in the cultural, educational and judicial spheres. Up to that year the local intelligentia was deeply soaked in Italian cultures and spirit. Italian was the language of the educated classes and it served as the language of the courts as well as the medium of instruction. An attack on Italian was considered as an attack on their social position. It is not surprising that the Commissioners' reports proved to be a watershed for Maltese politicians. These were roughly divided in two factions; those who supported the reforms and consequently were sympathetic to British rule in general and those who

were against. This issue (which later became known as "The Language Question") was the foundation stone of party politics in Malta.

The Reform Party and the *Partito Anti-Reformista* came into existence. The former was in favour of the proposed reforms and included among its supporters the people whose livelihood depended upon or was greatly enhanced by the presence of the British such as dockyard workers, merchants and those who looked upon Britain as a role model for future Malta. The latter included men of letters, the local clergy, the middle class in general especially lawyers who were the traditional leaders of the Maltese. The opposition was soon to utilise its majority in the Council (a majority catered for by the 1887 constitution) to block the influence of the English language primarily in schools.

The Language Question was not just a battle between English and Italian; it was only the tip of the iceberg. The main issue here was whether the British were to have complete control over education and Malta's historic links with Italy were to be broken for ever. The majority of the elected members were pro-Italians and they were going to do their best not to let what Britain dictated happen even to the detriment of progress in education. As a result of this situation an impasse was created when the Government's estimates to finance schools were not passed by the Council. In 1903, the 1887 Constitution was revoked and replaced by one whereby the elected members were in a minority.

But life in Malta during the 19th and 20th centuries was not only politics and constitutional ups and downs. The islands were visited from time to time by distinguished personalities such as King Edward VII, Lord Byron, Samuel Taylor

Dante Alighieri monument, Floriana, a testimony of the influence of italian culture in Malta.

Dun Karm's monument at Floriana.

Christ the King monument by Antonio Sciortino, Floriana.

Mtarfa naval hospital (detail).

Monument to the fallen in the Sette Giugno Riots in Valletta.

Mtarfa naval hospital.

Coleridge, Sir Walter Scott, D.H. Lawrence, Chesterton, Edward Lear and Benjamin Disraeli to mention but a few. Most of the British shipping in the Mediterranean called at the Grand Harbour for repairs or refuelling and Malta's congenial weather was highly recommended. Though tourism had not yet been developed into the industry that it is today, the islands had quite a reputation for relaxation.

A number of projects helped to modernise Malta and ease the life of its inhabitants such as the Victoria Gate (in Valletta) and a water distillation plant at Sliema. During the latter half of the 19th century a steam train operated between Valletta and Imdina facilitating transport between the new and old capitals of the island. Edward Middleton Barry designed the Royal Opera House which was built in Valletta and gave an invaluable boost to the artistic and cultural lives of the Maltese. Unfortunately, the Royal Opera House was hit by enemy fire and totally destroyed during the course of the Second World War.

The Eucharistic Congress of 1913 was a much celebrated event in which the Maltese participated with eagerness and enthusiasm. Cardinals and hundreds of high-ranking ecclesiastical officials attended the 24th International Congress which was held from the 23rd to the 27th April 1913. The bronze statue of Christ the King by the foremost Maltese sculptor Antonio Sciortino still adorns the Floriana square commonly referred to as *Il-Biskuttin* (The Biscuit) till this day. It represents the lofty figure of Christ at whose feet a woman wearing a crown made of bastions is kneeling. The human figure represents Malta and the statue symbolises the veneration which the Maltese still hold towards Our Lord.

Unfortunately the Eucharistic Congress did not manage to dissipate the hatred which had been gathering in human hearts. The following year, the First World War was raging and the Maltese displayed willingly their loyalty to the Crown even though the part played by the islands during this war was only marginal. All political rivalry was sus-

Life in the shelters, Mgarr.

pended until the end of the war. The French fleet was given permission to use Malta as its naval base and the dockyard was kept busy night and day to repair ships damaged by enemy action. The Germans had proclaimed unrestricted submarine warfare on Allied shipping and the Maltese did a good job at minesweeping. Over a thousand prisoners-of-war were kept at Salvatore Fort and Verdala Barracks whilst many injured sailors and troops from the military expedition at Gallipoli were nursed at the *Sacra Infermeria*, and the Mtarfa hospital, built in 1893. It is during these years that Malta maintained its reputation as the "Nurse of the Mediterranean".

With the end of the First World War, work at the dockyard (Malta's main industrial activity in those years) diminished drastically and unemployment was rife. Indeed, during the war years, there were about 10,000 workers at the dockyards alone.

With the end of the hostilities, many found themselves jobless and hundreds started to emigrate. The Maltese were used to this sort of fluctuation because the economy of the island boomed and slumped rhythmically according to the presence or absence of naval activity in the Mediterranean. A similar slump had been witnessed at the end of the Crimean War (1856) but the scale of the backlash after the First World War had been unprecedented.

The rise in the cost of living especially in the price of bread, the staple food of the islanders, as well as the Government's stern refusal to grant a legislative assembly made up of Maltese representatives, triggered the *Sette Giugno* Riots. Unrest in the capital city, on June 7th and 8th 1919 ended in bloodshed and the four major victims of the riots were revered as martyrs for the Maltese cause.

A monument to their memory was erected on their burial site, at the Adolorata Cemetery a few years after their death, whilst a more recent one, is seen at Palace Square. This incident was the worst that occurred between the British

Government and the local population. Luckily, good sense prevailed and further bloodshed was avoided. After some months of consultation with the chief political personalities led by Dr. (later Sir) Filippo Sceberras, a congenial constitution was granted in 1921.

The grant of Self Government was celebrated with joy and enthusiasm amongst the Maltese population. The first major political parties were set up and an election followed. It is ironic that the first Prime Minister of Malta, the businessman Joseph Howard, had an English surname.

The 1920's were a time when the Maltese began to explore their cultural roots. The inter-war years witnessed an interest in Maltese as a language. This was especially due to linguists such as Ninu Cremona and the ability of Dun Karm Psaila, the national poet, in whose hands the beauty of Maltese as a poetic medium was shown for the first time. It was during these years that Dun Karm composed a prayer to God beseeching the Almighty to protect the Maltese against evil and foster unity amongst them. A doctor and amateur musician by the name of Robert Samut composed the music to accompany this prayer which became so popular that it was adopted as the national anthem.

Greyish-black clouds were looming upon this idyllic atmosphere. The rise of the totalitarian regimes in Nazi Germany and Fascist Italy were disturbing the make-shift peace which had been created after the First World War. The policy-makers of the countries where democracy functioned could not sleep in peace as long as Hitler and Mussolini pursued their aggressive and expansionist ambitions. The Fascist dictator referred to Malta as *"terra irredenta"* (Unredeemed land) making his intentions of uniting the Maltese archipelago to Italy quite obvious. Although most Maltese politicians of the time looked favourably towards Italy (Italian was, up to 1934, the official language of the islands) it is not clear whether they were inclined towards integration with the peninsula. When the international situation was

School continues in the shelters, Mġarr.

Mosta Dome designed by Architect Grognet de Vasse.

getting out of hand, the British authorities in Malta rounded up a group of people who were either Italian sympathisers or suspected as being such. These Maltese from different social milieux ranging from judges to dockyard workers were deported to concentration camps in Uganda. One of them, Nerik Mizzi, was destined to become leader of the Nationalist Party and Prime Minister of Malta.

By 1939 the die was cast. With the entry of Italy in the war siding with the Axis, the Maltese knew that life was not going to be easy.

And so it was. On the very day that the *Duce* declared war, on June 11th 1940, Italian bombers attacked the islands, killing six Maltese soldiers at Fort St. Elmo. The Maltese endured their fate with epic heroism. Shelters were dug out of live rock and it was there that the civilian population waited for interminable hours whilst the enemy dropped tons of bombs destroying most of the houses in the harbour area.

The countryside was not spared its share of occasional raids. It was during one of these attacks, in 1942, that a thousand pound bomb penetrated the dome of the Rotunda at Mosta during the celebration of mass. Miraculously the bomb failed to explode and is preserved, to this very day, in the sacristy of the church. Malta was not sufficiently prepared for the war. To combat the raids of the Italian *Regia Aeronautica*, and later the Nazi *Luftwaffe*, the Maltese relied on anti-aircraft guns and three Gloster Gladiators adequately referred to as "Faith" "Hope", and "Charity".

One of them ("Faith") can still be seen at the National War Museum, housed at Fort St. Elmo. The award of the George Cross Medal by King George VI to the whole population of Malta was an acknowledgement of the nation's fortitude during this difficult period. The letter dated 15th April 1942, written and signed by the King himself, stated: "*To honour her brave people I award the George Cross to the Island Fortress of Malta to bear witness to a heroism and devotion that will long be famous in history.*"

The George Cross Medal was handed by the Governor Lord Gort to Chief Justice Sir George Borg who received it on behalf of the nation. Till this day, as embodied in the Maltese Constitution, the George Cross Medal appears on the top corner of the white canton on the Maltese flag.

The country was on the verge of starvation but the Maltese were serving as an example of unfailing courage and dogged determination. A turning point in the history of Malta during the Second World War was the arrival of the so-called "Santa Maria Convoy" on the 15th August 1942.

A convoy of 14 merchant vessels was sent to relieve the oppressed population. Although they were under heavy escort, the ships were bombarded so much that only five managed to limp into the Grand Harbour.

The Maltese were elated and welcomed the arrival of the ships with cries of joy from the top of the bastions. The ships not only gave the disheartened population a fresh boost of morale, they also carried sufficient provisions to ward off starvation and continue the struggle till milder times.

After the war there was an intense period of reconstruction especially in Valletta and the Three Cities. Self-Government was restored but, during the fifties, the Maltese began to crave for two possible alternatives; either complete integration with Great Britain (an idea championed by the Malta Labour Party) or Independence (as proposed by the Nationalist Party).

Eventually the scheme for integration was abandoned and Independence within the Commonwealth was achieved on the 21st September 1964.

On the 13th December 1974 Malta was declared a democratic Republic and five years later, on the 31st March 1979 the Military Base Agreement was terminated. The last British Warship, HMS *London*, left the Grand Harbour on the 1st April 1979, 180 years after the *Northumberland* and the *Culloden* had first entered that same harbour to help a population in distress.

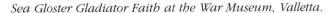

Sea Gloster Gladiator Faith at the War Museum, Valletta.

R.A.F. memorial, Floriana.

Reminders of the British era - red letter box in Valletta.

Lascaris war rooms.

Lascaris war rooms where enemy action was monitored.

Monument commemorating Independence Day at Floriana.

PROTESTANT PLACES OF WORSHIP

The difference in the religious beliefs and traditions between the Maltese and their British overlords was one of the two factors which could mar an otherwise blissful relationship between the rulers and the ruled. The other factor was the English language which was used and understood by practically nobody on the arrival of the British troops in 1798-99.

The fear that the British would attempt to convert substantial sections of the population to Protestantism was a constant worry looming at the back of the ecclesiastical authorities' minds.

The Bishops of Malta (even the most pro-British) with the help of parish priests monitored what was happening with watertight scrutiny.

On the other hand, the British knew how sensitive the Maltese were about religious matters and, wishing to maintain excellent relations with their newly acquired subjects, tried to appease the local Roman Catholic ecclesiastic authorities as much as possible. This sometimes led to embarrassing situations.

The first Governor of "Malta and its dependencies", Sir Thomas Maitland refused to let the Bible Society of Malta distribute translations of the Protestant version of the Bible. Maitland was also instructed by the Secretary of State to refuse:

"upon any account, (to) occupy the Church of St. John as a place of Protestant worship... Nor do I consider it advisable to appropriate any church which is in the use of the Catholic Inhabitants to the service of the English residents.

It appears to me to be far more advisable to enlarge the existing chapel in the Palace and continue to make use of that building as the Place of Worship for persons of the Protestant faith."

It is clear that this state of affairs was not satisfactory to the increasing number of English residents who wanted to practise their faith. However this situation was maintained till the arrival of the Queen dowager, Adelaide, widow of the late King William IV and the aunt of Queen Victoria, in November 1838. She was definitely not pleased with this *modus vivendi* and decided to erect a church contributing the huge sum of 10,000 pounds sterling to cater for its expenses.

The foundation stone was laid by Queen Adelaide herself on the 20th March 1839 and work was terminated five years later in 1844 after a temporary suspension owing to defective construction. The site of the Church at *Piazza Celsi* (today's Independence Square) was previously occupied by the German Auberge.

On November 1, 1844 the building was consecrated by the Bishop of Gibraltar, Reverend George Tomlinson, and was dedicated to St. Paul.

Other places of Protestant worship are Holy Trinity Church at Sliema, and the Wesleyan Church at Floriana which has been converted into an exhibition hall known as Robert Samut Hall. Designed by Thomas Mallett Ellis, the Wesleyan Church was built in March 1883 and its opening was spectacular since it was one of the very first occasions where incandescent lamps were used. Next to this church one finds what was once the "Connaught Home for Sailors and Soldiers".

The foundation stone of this building was laid by the Duke of Connaught on the 30th March 1908.

The most interesting feature about Protestant churches in Malta is that even architecturally they provide a striking contrast with the baroque Roman Catholic Churches.

Queen Victoria – A monarch in Republic Square.

In the Msida Bastion one finds the main Protestant burial place from 1806 to circa 1856. In this small cemetery in the bastion many Protestants were buried until another burial place was found at Ta' Braxia (also known as Pietà Military Cemetery) not far away. Happily, the Msida Bastion Cemetery has been recently restored by Din l-Art Helwa after a long period of abandonment in which it was almost totally dilapidated. Today the place has been transformed into a Garden of Rest and is open to the public. Recently, Europa Nostra has awarded a Medal of Honour to Din l-Art Helwa for this rehabilitation project.

Ensign at the Pro-Cathedral, Valletta.

St. Paul's Pro-Cathedral, Valletta.

Interior of St. Paul's Pro-Cathedral, Valletta.

Ta' Braxia cemetery, Pietà.

Holy Trinity Church, Sliema.

A Queen's Monument in Republic Square

The statue of Queen Victoria, which ironically one finds in the centre of Republic Square, is the work of the Sicilian sculptor Giuseppe Valente. It was unveiled by Lady Smyth, the Lieutenant-Governor's wife, on the 5th August 1891 following the celebrations to commemorate the Queen's fiftieth jubilee. The financing of the statue was done through public subscription.

The seated queen is wearing a shawl of Malta lace (or *"bizzilla"*). Lace-making is an ancient craft handed down from mother to daughter. Unfortunately this craft has practically died out but, with some luck, one can still see some old women fumbling their pegs (*"ċombini"*) in certain villages in Gozo. The association with Queen Victoria stems from the fact that the monarch had ordered *"eight dozen pairs long and eight dozen pairs short mitts, besides a scarf..."* in an attempt to revive this ancient craft. The marble statue of the Queen replaced the

Statue of Queen Victoria unveiled on August 5th 1891.

Traditional lace-making.

bronze statue of Grand Master Antonio Manoel de Vilhena which can still be seen today in Floriana.

Although the square is officially known as Republic Square, the Maltese commonly refer to it as *Pjazza Reġina* (Queen's Square). At the back of the statue one finds the National Library while to its right there is the President's Palace where the Maltese Parliament holds its sittings. The celebrations in honour of Queen Victoria were often an occasion for a public show of loyalty to Britain. It is interesting to note that the Gozitans, led by their Bishop Paul Pace, requested the town of Rabat to be given city status and that it should bear the name Victoria.

This request was granted on the 10th June 1887.

SA MAISON GARDEN

On the counterguard of San Salvatore, overlooking the picturesque Pietà creek within the Marsamxett Harbour, there is the beautiful garden known as Sa Maison or *Il-Gnien tal-Milorda* (Milady's Garden).

Originally the site of Chevallier Caille Maison's hunting lodge, the place was rented to Lady Julia Lockwood in 1842 for an annual rent of 40 pounds sterling (1). The new owner took great pains to improve the house and embellish the adjoining gardens. However, with the mounting tension in the Balkans (which eventually led to the Crimean War), the site proved to be indispensable for military operations and it was requested by the Authorities. In 1852 the Civil Government wanted Lady Julia to give up the house and after a protracted correspondence, the owner had to give in. In 1856 Sa Maison was passed on to the Military. Many British regiments used the garden from time to time, leaving their regimental badges hewn in the bastion's rock. Of particular interest is the Castle of Gibraltar, erected in 1899 by the 56th Foot 2nd Battalion, Essex Regiment (2). The breathtaking view from the watch tower, together with the peaceful atmosphere that envelops this garden within walking distance from the capital city makes it a place worth visiting.

REFERENCE

(1) Guze' Cassar Pullicino, "Il-Gnien tal-Milorda", Heritage, pp. 196-200

(2) Joseph Borg, "The Public Gardens and Groves of Malta and Gozo", pp. 63-65

Rock-cut regimental coat of arms – Sa Maison.

Rock-cut regimental coat of arms – Sa Maison.

*The Castle of Gibraltar at
Sa Maison Gardens.*

The Harbour area.

Lions' Fountain at Sa Maison.

Gardens as Gifts

Sa Maison is not the only garden which reminds us of the British administration of the Maltese islands. Luqa Briffa Garden is small yet beautiful in the town of Żejtun. Named after a Maltese hero during the Turkish siege of Malta in 1565, the garden is also known as *"il-Ġnien tal-Luktenent"* (Lieutenant's Garden).

The commemorative marble inscription on its main entrance reads: *"This garden, completely constructed during the Administration of Knight and Baron Alexander John Ball, on behalf of King George III of Britain, Governor of the Island of Malta and Gozo for the use of the present and future inhabitants of this village."*

On this inscription one also finds a crowned Royal monogram; GR (Georgius Rex) resting on the British banner, all carved in the typical globigerina limestone.

Ball seems to have been conscious of the lack of greenery especially in the island of Malta. On his initiative various botanic gardens were planted in villages such as Safi and Gudja.

Trees were also planted in what proved to be a major afforestation project (1). In the small village of Għargħur, besides the botanic garden, a house was built to accommodate the lieutenant. The house is known as *"Il-Palazz tal-Kmand"* (The Commander's

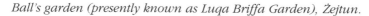

Ball's garden (presently known as Luqa Briffa Garden), Żejtun.

QUESTO GIARDINO FU COMINCIATO E TERMINATO
SOTTO L AMMINISTRAZIONE DEL CAV E BARONETTO
ALESSANDRO GIOVANNI BALL
PER
GIORGIO TERZO
RE DELLA GRAN BRETTAGNA
GOVERNANTE
LE ISOLE DI MALTA E GOZO
AL USO DEI LUOGOTENNTI TEMPORANEI DE   LI
IL LUOGO E IN PERPETUO CONSECRATO

Details showing Coat of Arms (Georgius Rex) King George at the façade of the recently restored Luqa Briffa Garden, Żejtun.

Palace). It seems that Ball wanted to reward the leaders of the Maltese insurgents against the French without whose help and trust Britain would not have received the heartfelt welcome of the rest of the population.

Garden by Alexander Ball at Safi.

REFERENCE
(1) Michael Galea, Sir Alexander John Ball and Malta, 1990, p.112

Interior of garden, Safi.

Ball's garden at Gudja.

One of Ball's garden's at Għargħur.

Having an empty built on the navy, the British immediately realised the strategic importance of the Maltese islands. From the Order of St. John, they had inherited a fortified harbour equipped with an efficient dockyard operating from one of its creeks. At a time when the Mediterranean was infested with pirates and Muslim corsairs it was unwise to provide coastal lighting and so, during the Order's rule, a lighthouse in the star-shaped fort St. Elmo as well as a beacon on the hill known as Tal-Ġurdan in Gozo provided the only solace for the guidance of friendly shipping. During the mid-19th century the situation improved through the efforts of two enthusiastic administrators. In 1850, Governor Richard More O'Ferrall commissioned the building of a lighthouse at Delimara, a project completed five years later. This provided a steady mark for seafarers in the east and south-eastern waters and was greatly appreciated especially by the fishermen of Marsaxlokk. On the 11th October 1857, O'Ferrall's successor, Sir William Reid (himself an able scientist) officially opened a lighthouse at Tal-Ġurdan which is still in operation today after having its lighting apparatus modernised in 1963 (1). The harbour area was well-provided for. Besides the lighthouse at St. Elmo, another one was erected on the other side of the harbour's entrance at Fort Ricasoli in the limits of Kalkara. These two posts, however, became redundant when the breakwaters project was terminated in the early years of the 20th century. They were replaced by lights at the end of the breakwaters.

REFERENCE
(1) Joseph Borg, "Maltese Landmarks; the Lighthouses", Heritage, pp.227-230

The majestic baroque façade of Fort Ricasoli.

Beacons in the dark, Delimara lighthouse – limits of Marsaxlokk.

BIGHI HOSPITAL

In 1814, the British came to possess not a barren, useless rock but a strategically important island with a prosperous and diligent population whose only desire was to live in peace under the Sovereign's protection. The Knights of St. John had left a well-fortified island and their presence had bolstered the artistic and cultural milieu of the inhabitants. Rich knights owned villas in which they could relax far away from the hectic life of the city. One such knight was Fra Giovanni Bichi who built Villa Bichi on the promontory of Kalkara with a splendid view of the Grand Harbour. Later the villa passed on to his nephew Fra Mario. The site's connection with Britain dates back to 1753 when the villa became the residence of the British Consul in Malta, John Dodsworth. Half a century later, in 1803, it caught Admiral Nelson's attention who pinpointed the building as an ideal spot on which to build a naval hospital. He wrote:

"I suppose the Admiralty, if we are to keep the troops at Malta, will establish a proper naval hospital... the large house on the Bichi headland would be a very fit place for a marine hospital."

The first mention of the house being used as a hospital is in 1813 when Bichi (or Bighi) Palace catered for the needs of the plague-stricken victims of the Cottonera area. The erection of the wing adjacent to the villa cost 20,000 pounds sterling. The foundation stone of the new building was laid by Vice-Admiral Sir Putteney Malcolm on the 23rd March 1830. When the works were completed, Bichi Palace was, in actual fact, converted into a hospital with the capacity for treating around 300 patients. For many years the hospital served the Admiralty until it was handed over to the Maltese Government in September 1970. The building served as a secondary school and is now in the process of being converted into a tech-

Villa Bighi – a naval hospital at the entrance of the Grand Harbour.

Villa Bighi. The construction through which patients were taken from the shore to the hospital.

nology complex. The other hospital in the harbour area was the Military Hospital in Vittoriosa, built in 1873 during the administration of Governor Sir Charles Thomas Van Straubenzee. Years later, Lord Gerald Strickland converted the premises into a college, a role which it still performs today.

The Maritime Museum & the Hibernia

Originally the site of the Order's dockyard, the naval bakery was built in 1845 after the yards were scrapped three years earlier in order to set up the Victualling Yard. The naval bakery, designed by architect William Scamp, catered for the production of bread and biscuits which used to be supplied to the British warships harboured in Malta. Owing to the large amounts of dough which had to be prepared daily, steam-propelled engines were used and the ovens were quite huge. One can just imagine the fragrant odour of freshly baked bread which used to linger in the nearby streets!

After the termination of the British naval base in 1979, the building was left unused until it was wonderfully restored and converted into a Maritime museum in 1992. A visit to this museum is very much worthwhile. Two allegorical oil paintings by Ramiro Calì (one representing Malta and the other the British Empire) adorn the staircase of the building. Amongst the most treasured exhibits found in the museum is the *HMS Hibernia*'s figurehead representing the Irish-Celtic idol Dogda. Launched at Plymouth Dockyard on the 17th November 1804, the *HMS Hibernia* spent most of her active life in the Mediterranean, becoming the base flagship for Malta in 1855. The *Hibernia*'s presence at Dockyard Creek near Fort St. Angelo became the symbol of the close links between the Royal Navy and Malta especially with the people of the Three Cities (Vittoriosa, Cospicua, and Senglea). Eventually the ship was scrapped but, for a time, the wooden figurehead decorating its bows was displayed at the entrance of Fort St. Angelo. In 1974 it was returned to Britain where it stood outside the Victory Museum at Portsmouth. However, in November 1994, it was officially handed over to the Maritime Museum as a token of the ever-lasting friendship between the two islands - a friendship which began and was forged by the sea.

REFERENCE
Antonio Espinosa Rodriguez,
The Malta Maritime Museum,
Malta tourism Authority.

Royal Coat of Arms at Maritime Museum, at Vittoriosa.

Figurehead of HMS Hibernia.

Model of the Order's galley used for naval instruction at Maritime Museum, Vittoriosa.

Bell at "HMS St. Angelo".

Fort. St. Angelo. A fort and a battleship.

Villa Rundle Garden

When Sir Henry Macleod Leslie Rundle became governor in 1909 the economic situation of the islands was not a bright one. Works on the breakwaters were terminated and many had found themselves unemployed.

The situation was so desperate that a Royal Commission was appointed in 1911 to give a full report on the financial and economic conditions of Malta. Notwithstanding this gloomy picture, Sir Leslie's governorship was marked with many great occasions such as the Royal visit of King George V and Queen Mary in 1912 and the 24th International Eucharistic Congress held in Malta the following year. The gardens which adorn the capital of Gozo were laid out by Sir Leslie and officially opened to the public in 1915.

Although Gozo is greener than Malta, the opening of the Villa Rundle gar-

Preceding pages:
Vittoriosa. The Maritime Museum, St. Lawrence Collegiate Church and Freedom Monument.

Fountain at Villa Rundle, Gozo.

Villa Rundle, Victoria Gozo.

dens was a much-awaited event since the sister isle did not enjoy recreational spaces such as the Upper and Lower Barraccas and San Anton Gardens.

The Rundle gardens at Victoria proved to be an invaluable venue for activities such as the annual agricultural exhibition organised by the Gozo Agricultural, Industrial and Cultural Society. In the gardens one also finds the busts of distinguished Gozitans such as the lexicographer Gianpiet Agius de Soldanis and the poet Laurent Ropa.

BALL'S MONUMENT

In the Lower Barracca, in the nation's capital, there is a small neo-classical monument dedicated to the man who was instrumental in fostering a deep understanding between the Maltese and the British. Sir Alexander John Ball was appointed Civil Commissioner when Malta came under British protection.

He was held in high esteem by a population whose sole wish was to form part of the British Empire. On the occasion of his departure from Malta on the 4th September 1802, the representatives of the Maltese had presented him with a sword as a token of their gratitude and affection. Unfortunately the sword was stolen and another one was given to him later on. Ball had, in fact, been chiefly responsible for uniting the Maltese leaders and forming an organised common front against the French blockaded in the harbour cities. Due to his experience in dealing with the inhabitants, Sir Alexander Ball was sent to Malta and of-ficially succeeded Charles Cameron as Civil Commissioner in May 1803. With the resumption of hostilities the importance of the islands became increasingly evident.

Sir Alexander Ball died in office on the 25th October 1809 at San Anton Palace which, during his stay, had served as his quarters and residence. He was buried in a ravelin in Fort St. Elmo where an inscription is still visible today. The site of the monument was chosen by Edmund Francis Chapman, Civil Commissioner ad interim, because it was *"a fortified spot commanding the sea... specially adapted to be the tomb of a hero..."*

The monument itself, the work of Maltese architect, Giorgio Pullicino, was funded by contributions from the Maltese and his friends. The work is in the neo-classical style. Statues representing Wisdom and Immortality adorn it.

Other Governors such as Thomas Maitland and Francis Rawdon, the Marquis of Hastings, have their monuments erected in other gardens in Valletta.

Fort St. Angelo, Birgu, withheld innumerable enemy attacks during World War II.

Monument to Sir Alexander Ball, Lower Baracca, Valletta.

Maitland's simple memorial at the Upper Barracca reflects the unpopularity of the first despotic Lieutenant Governor of the islands. In front of the Governor's Palace in Valletta, on the building known as The Main Guard, the tablet under the coat of arms of Britain reminds the onlooker that the British were governing through the love of the Maltese and the consent of Europe. Maitland, however, did not seem to give much consideration to the monument (built, ironically, during his own administration) and ruled with an iron fist. Appropriately known as "King Tom" his demise on January 17th 1824 was largely unmourned.

Maitland's successor, the Marquis of Hastings, was more humane and during his brief two year administration (1824-26) he did much to alleviate the hardships of the populace. Hastings' marble memorial at Hastings Gardens in Valletta consists of a pediment on four columns. A statue of the Marquis lies in a reclining position. Though a kind-hearted person, the Marquis was something of an eccentric.

In a letter found amongst his private belongings, he expressed the wish that upon his death his right hand be cut off and preserved, later to be buried with his wife.

Sir Frederick Cavendish Ponsonby is another Governor whose memorial is found in Hastings Gardens. A 21 metre-high column had been erected in his honour in 1838 but on the 11th January 1864 it was destroyed after being hit by lightning. Today only the base of this column is visible.

A garden on the bastions: Hasting's garden, Valletta.

Monument to the Marquis of Hastings, Valletta.

At Blata l-Bajda's flyover one finds the monument dedicated to the Honourable Sir Robert Spencer which was originally erected at Corradino. In the obituary appearing in the Malta Government Gazette of 24th November 1830, Sir Robert Cavendish Spencer (1791-1830) was described as *a distinguished officer and an excellent man*.

During his short life, he distinguished himself in commanding various naval vessels. For a while he lived in Malta which was, at the time, governed by his cousin Sir Frederick Cavendish Ponsonby. He was also known for the lavish parties which he threw for his friends, where wine was never lacking.

The monument itself, in the shape of an obelisk, is the work of architect Giorgio Pullicino, who was also responsible for Ball's monument at the Lower Barracca. Pullicino has been credited as one of the early exponents of neo-classical architecture in Malta. The monument was set up by the officers, seamen, and marines of H.M.S. Madagascar, the ship under Spencer's command when he died off Alexandria on the 4th November 1830. The captain was buried at St. Michael's Bastion in Valletta. In March 1893 the monument was transferred to its present site owing to the exigencies of work in that side of the harbour.

Commemorative plaque at base of Spencer monument.

74

Further Reading
Michael Ellul, "National Monuments;
Spencer's monument, Blata l-Bajda",
Heritage vol. 57, pp.1124-1127

Spencer monument, Blata l-Bajda.

Mnajdra Temple in the Vicinity of Congreve Memorial.

CONGREVE MEMORIAL

The memorial slab found a short distance away from the Mnajdra Temple is almost imperceptible because of its simplicity and smallness. However the unimposing Congreve memorial tells the story of a man who came to the islands as their Governor and ended up falling deeply in love with this friendly nation and peaceful environment. The inscription on the slab reads as follows:
"Sacred to the memory
Of His Excellency
Sir Walter Norris Congreve
VC, KCB, MVO
Governor of Malta
Buried at Sea on the 4th March 1927
Between this spot and Filfla Island."

Sir Walter Norris Congreve was a veteran of the South African War and during the First World War his left hand had been amputated and replaced by a silver hook. When he was appointed Governor, Malta had recently been granted a comparatively liberal constitution which allowed a considerable degree of self-government. Consequently Congreve found himself in a lucky administrative position where no major antagonistic decision had to be taken. As a result during the three years of his Governorship (1924-1927) Sir Walter was loved and respected for his amiable character. However, his health was not optimal and it continued to deteriorate until the 28th February 1927, the day of his death at Imtarfa Hospital. The corpse was taken to St. Paul's Pro-Cathedral where it was laid in state. On the 4th March, according to his last wishes, Sir Walter was taken on board the frigate *HMS Chrysanthemum* and buried at sea. The funeral cortege included the then Prime Minister of Malta, Sir Ugo Mifsud, and various members of the Council of Government.

Congreve Memorial with Filfla in the background.

THE RAF MALTA MEMORIAL

In Floriana, a short distance away from City Gate, one finds an impressive memorial dedicated to the memory of the airmen who lost their lives in combat during World War II. On a bronze tablet at the monument's base one reads this inscription:

"Over these and
Neighbouring
Lands and Seas
The Airmen
Whose names are
Recorded here
fell in raid or
sortie and have
no known grave
MALTA / GIBRALTAR / MEDITERRANEAN /
ADRIATIC / TUNISIA / SICILY / ITALY /
YUGOSLAVIA / AUSTRIA

Propositi Insula   *For this the Island*
Tenax Tenaces   *commemorates*
Viros   *the Bravest of the*
Commemorat"   *Brave.*

On the other nineteen tablets there are the names of the airmen from New Zealand, Canada, Australia, South Africa and the UK arranged according to year of death, force and rank. The printed register of names is kept at the British High Commission. The marble memorial consists of a round base and a decorated column on top of which there is the symbol of the RAF - an eagle standing on a globe. The RAF motto "PER ARDUA AD ASTRA" is inscribed at the base of the column.

Temple of Mnajdra a short distance
away from Ħaġar Qim,
and Congreve Memorial.

Milestone in the country-side - the distance to Valletta was erased during World War II for security reasons.

War memorial, Floriana unveiled on November 11th 1938.

THE WAR MEMORIAL

In the vicinity of the RAF Malta Memorial, one can find the War Memorial. Built in the form of a Latin cross, this memorial was unveiled on the 11th November 1938 by the Governor General Sir Charles Bonham-Carter. The monument's original site was further up St. Anne's Street in Floriana. Every Armistice Day, flowers are laid by its sides. A bronze wreath at the foot of the monument provides a perpetual remembrance to those who have fallen during the two World Wars. Messages from King George VI and President Theodore Roosevelt pay homage to the brave and are found at the memorial's base.

THE VICTORIA LINES

Between 1870 and 1899, a feat of intense military importance was being undertaken at the North-Western side of Malta. Built on the edge of the ridge of a natural fault known as "The Great Fault" there is a series of fortifications extending from Fomm ir-Rih to Madliena Heights.

Originally referred to as the North-West Front, the wall was later renamed the Victoria Lines in honour of Queen Victoria, who celebrated her diamond jubilee in 1897.

The plaque which was unveiled at Targa Gap in 1897 reads as follows:
"The Victoria Lines
constructed during the administration
of His Excellency
General Sir Arthur Lyon
Fremantle
were so named
to commemorate the
Diamond Jubilee
of Her Majesty 1897"

The fortifications comprise various battery posts, gun emplacements and four forts; Fort Bingemma, Fort Mosta, Fort Madliena, and Fort Pembroke.

The Victoria Lines defending the North-West side of Malta.

Entrance to Mosta Fort.

Plaque commemorating the construction of the Victoria Lines 1897.

Mosta Fort ditch.

Mosta Fort, in defence of the Victoria Lines.

Live interpretation displays by enthusiasts.

FORT RINELLA – KALKARA

The British military authorities increasingly realised that the innumerable fortifications which the Order of St. John had built throughout their rule over the islands were not adequate to resist attacks by more powerful and accurate artillery.

Their importance was next to nothing had they not been equipped with heavy guns. As a result of such a realisation between 1876 and 1884, a fort was built at Wied Ghammieq in the limits of Kalkara to complement Fort Ricasoli at the tip of the Grand

Harbour facing Fort St. Elmo.

The most notable feature of this fort is the 100 ton gun with a calibre of 45 cm. This gigantic gun used to fire shells at a range of 6 km and its only twin is found in Gibraltar.

The fort also has accommodation quarters for the garrisoned troops. Drills and garrison life are periodically re-enacted in the fort by amateur actors wearing late Victorian army uniforms.

Round about the same period, other Point Batteries and forts were being built at Sliema. The fort at Għar id-Dud (the popular Sliema promenade) was completed in 1876 and is presently used as an eatery.

The thousand pound bomb which pierced the Mosta Rotunda during an air raid in 1942.

Sliema Point Battery at Ghar id-Dud, Sliema.

Massive 100 ton gun at Fort Rinella.

Fort Rinella, Re-furbished interior rooms.

THE FAWWARA AQUEDUCT

Prior to the use of reverse osmosis plants, the adequate supply of potable water was always a source of worry especially during the dry seasons. Between 1610 and 1615, when the islands were governed by the Order of St. John, Grand Master Alof de Wignacourt authorised the construction of an aqueduct which stretched from Attard to Sta. Venera. As a result of this project, fresh water could be supplied to the otherwise dry city of Valletta.

The importance of using natural water springs to the maximum was evident to one and all. For this reason, during 1844-45, an aqueduct was built at Fawwara in the limits of Siġġiewi, a picturesque village in the south-western part of Malta. The word "fawwara" itself means a spring of rising water, and there are other places in Malta and Gozo bearing this name. Towards the end of the 19th century, when the supply of water was constantly meagre, the Cottonera district was provided with water from the spring found in this area.

Problems related to the shortage of water began to be felt once again, owing to the ever-growing population which needed larger amounts of water, and to periodic droughts. The little rainfall in 1866 was the cause of the distress felt in many villages and towns in the same year. Fresh water had to be supplied by casks in many villages. Towns such as Sliema, which, towards the end of the 19th century, were developing at a fast rate, had to find ways and means to cater for their needs. In 1881 a Sea Water Distilling Apparatus was built in Sliema, close to the Tigne' quarters. It is still visible today and used as a printing press. The bronze statue which we find in the small space in front of the Balluta Buildings in Balluta originally was at St. Anne's square in Sliema. It commemorates the extension of the water supply to Sliema in 1882, a project carried out during the administration of Sir Arthur Borton. Architect Emmanuel L. Galizia was the superintendent of public works who supervised the project. Governor Borton may also be remembered as the Governor during whose administration San Anton Gardens were opened to the general public.

Fawwara aqueduct, Siġġiewi.

Details of fountain commemorating the extension of water supply to Sliema.

San Anton Palace opened to the public by Governor Sir Arthur Borton

Fountain at San Anton Gardens built during the Grand Mastership of Fra Antoine de Paule.

Diana's fountain at San Anton.

Victoria Gate, Valletta detail.

Preceding pages:
Fawwara Acqueduct at Siġġiewi.

THE VICTORIA GATE

The main gates of Valletta, which were suitable enough for the Knights, were not so adequate for the exigencies of the 19th and 20th centuries. They had to be enlarged to ensure an easier flow of traffic in and out of the city. In 1854, Laparelli's main gate was reconstructed and renamed "Kingsgate". The construction was very artistic but in 1964 it was replaced again by the present "Citygate" designed by architect Bergonzi. Towards the end of the 19th century, what used to be known as *Porta del Monte* (named after Grand Master Pietro del Monte) or *Porta Marina* was demolished and subsequently built again comprising two entrances. The work was carried out in 1884 and the foundation stone of the new project was laid by Sir Arthur Borton on May 27th 1884.

Victoria Gate was designed by Emmanuel L. Galizia. The coats of arms of Malta and Valletta are on the two main arched entrances whilst Britain's provides a very decorative frontispiece.

A similar fate befell the *Portes des Bombes* in Floriana. Originally built by architect Mondion under the Grand Mastership of Ramon Perellos, the gate was enlarged by constructing a symmetrical arch on the other side of the existing one. The project was carried out by engineer Dunford and was completed on the 17th August 1868. The inscription on the "new" arch reads; *"Ad Majorem Popoli Commoditatem"* ("For the Greater Convenience of the People" 1868).

Victoria Gate Valletta. The foundation stone was laid by Sir Arthur Borton on May 27th 1884.

THE GEORGE CROSS

Article 3 of the Constitution of Malta states that;

"(1) The National Flag of Malta consists of two equal vertical stripes, white in the hoist and red in the fly.
(2) A representation of the George Cross awarded to Malta by His Majesty King George the Sixth on the 15th April, 1942 is carried, edged with red, in the canton of the white stripe."

In 1942 Malta was in the centre of aerial attacks by the *Luftwaffe* and the *Regia Aeronautica*.

The Maltese were psychologically at a low ebb as a result of daily bombardment which destroyed their capital city Valletta and other cities around the harbour. Vittoriosa, Senglea and Cospicua were almost totally devastated due to their vicinity to the drydocks in the Grand Harbour. But the blitzed people were not to be beaten. The Maltese sought safety in shelters dug into live rock and thousands of refugees from the harbour area were housed in the homes of their compatriots living in the villages. The major problem was supply. The overpopulated islands depended on the importation of foodstuffs from other countries.

The supply lines were severely jeopardised due to attacks and conditions were so precarious that Governor Gort considered the surrender of Malta to the enemy.

In the midst of these circumstances, the King sent his honour together with a short message read to the Maltese people by their Governor.

The message stated:
"The Governor
*   Malta*
*   To honour her brave people I award the George Cross to the Island Fortress of Malta to bear witness to a heroism and devotion that will long be famous in history.*
*   April 15th 1942*
*   George R.I."*

Rarely did thirty-one simple words have such an impact on the morale of a whole nation. On September 13th, 1942, General Lord Gort presented the George Cross to the Chief Justice, Sir George Borg. The formal ceremony took place in

Maltese flag hoisted on top of Auberge de Castille.
During World War II, the Auberge served as Military Headquarters.

War Museum, entrance to shelter, dug out in live rock.

War Museum at Fort St. Elmo, Valletta.

the Main Guard in front of the Governor's Palace in Valletta. It was a brief but significant event and it did a lot to boost the morale of a people who had commended their destiny to the mercy of God.

Relief had come a few weeks earlier when a big convoy had managed to arrive safely in Malta bringing the desperately-needed provisions. Although heavily bombarded, the convoy "Ohio" managed to enter the Grand Harbour to the jubilation of the islanders. The Maltese got what they needed to sustain resistance till victory.

To this day the little cross on every Maltese flag is a constant reminder of the time when Malta had to face its darkest hour. It is a reminder to every Maltese that during the struggle against Fascism and Nazism, the islanders had done their duty with valour.

War Museum, Valletta. Grim reminder of the destruction of the harbour area.

49 to Ghajin Tuffieha
48 to Cirkewwa via Ghadira
51 to Sliema ferry via Coast Road
70 to Rabat via Mosta and Ta'Qali
86 to Marsaxlokk
427

Bahar
68 ic-Caghaq

St.Andrews

Gharghur
55
67,671
672
St.Julian's/Paceville

Naxxar
54,56
Ta'Giorni 66
Sliema 60 61
70
San Gwann 62 ★

to Bugiba Qawra via Coast Road
to Rabat via St.Julians, Taz-Zwejt,
Mosta and Ta'Qali

Mosta
53,57
Taz-Zwejt Gzira

VALLETTA
terminus

Lija
Balzan
40
Birkirkara Msida/Pieta
71,78
41,42
Ferry
Floriana

Kalkara
Vittoriosa 4
1, 2, 6

Xghajra
23 to Cospicua

Corinthia
Palace 74
San Anton
Gardens
St. Venera
Senglea 3
Cospicua
22 to Marsascala
23 to Xghajra
28 to Zejtun

San
Leonardo

Ta'Qali

Attard
Hamrun

MALTA
Qormi
90,91
Marsa
18,21 Zabbar

Sliema ferry via Ta'Qali, Mosta,
Taz-Zwejt and St.Julian's
Xemxija
Bugiba via Mosta and Ta'Qali

Zebbug
88

St.Vincent 37
de Paule

Paola
Fgura

Tarxien

Marsaskala
19
22 to Cospicua

Luqa
36

Siggiewi 89
94

to Ghar Lapsi
(summer only)

LUQA AIRPORT

15
Santa Lucia

Zejtun
26,29
28 to Cospicua

St.Thomas
Bay 29
St.Thomas Bay

8 Gudja&
Ghaxaq

Mqabba
Kirkop

Marsaxlokk
27
427 to Bugiba

Orendi 35
Safi

Birzebbuga
11,115
Marsaxlokk
Bay

Ghar Lapsi
94
Zurrieq
32,34,39

Hal Far
13

Kalafrana
12

to Siggiewi
(summer only)

Car ferry Mgarr-Sliema

Car ferry Valletta-Sicillia

Grand Harbour

St Lukes Hospital 75

BIBLIOGRAPHY

A.E. Abela, Governors of Malta, Progress Press 1991
Joseph Borg, The Public Gardens and Groves of Malta and Gozo, Media Centre 1990
Ray Cachia Zammit, ed., The Victoria Lines; souvenir guide, 1997
Michael Galea, Sir Alexander John Ball, Publishers Enterprises Group 1990
Alfie Gaullaumier, *Bliet u Irħula Maltin*, vols. 1,2,3., Valletta Publishing 1992
Jesmond Grech, *Malta Taħt l-Ingliżi*, Klabb Kotba Maltin 1997
R.G. Kirkpatrick, St. Paul's Anglican Pro-Cathedral; Valletta, Malta G.C., 1988
A.V. Laferla; British Malta, vols. 1,2., A.C. Aquilina 1976
Various articles from Heritage,
Margaret Weaver, Holy Trinity Church; Sliema Malta G.C., 1988
A.N.Welsh, The Msida Bastion Garden of Rest, 1995
Joseph M. Brincat, Malta 870-1054 Al-Himyari's Account, Said International 1991
Victor Mallia-Milanes (ed.), The British Colonial Experience 1800-1964, Mireva 1988
Henry Frendo, Malta's Quest for Independence, Valletta Publishing 1989
Joseph Attard, Britain and Malta; the story of an Era, Publishers Enterprises Group 1988
Herbert Ganado, *Rajt Malta Tinbidel*, vol. 2, Malta 1977

About the author

The son of a Royal Navy Petty Officer, Jesmond Grech was born at Imtarfa Naval Hospital in September 1963, a year before Malta achieved its Independence. He holds a Bachelorship and a Masters in Education from the University of Malta and teaches Maltese and European History at one of the State's Junior Lyceums. Grech is the author of "Malta Taħt l-Ingliżi" (Malta under the British), numerous articles, novels and several children's books. He is married to Mary and has two children, Julian and Cristina.

© Copyright by CASA EDITRICE PERSEUS collection PLURIGRAF
Published and printed by Centro Stampa Editoriale, Sesto Fiorentino, (Fi).